a b c

This book belongs to

....

Colour the star when
you complete a page.
See how far you've come!

4 5 6 7 8

9 10 11 12 13

14 15 16 17 18

19 20 21 22 23

Author: Carol Medcalf

How to use this book

- Find a quiet, comfortable place to work, away from distractions.

- This book has been written in a logical order, so start at the first page and work your way through.

- Help with reading the instructions where necessary and ensure that your child understands what to do.

- This book is a gentle introduction to 26 of the 44 sounds of the English language. Working through this book, your child will start to realise that words are made up of small separate sounds. These individual sounds are called phonemes; bus, for example, is made up of three phonemes: b-u-s. Encourage your child to say the individual letter sounds and to sound-blend to make words.

- If an activity is too difficult for your child then do more of our suggested practical activities (see Activity note) and return to the page when you know that they're likely to achieve it.

- Always end each activity before your child gets tired so they will be eager to return next time.

- Help and encourage your child to check their own answers as they complete each activity.

- Let your child return to their favourite pages once they have been completed. Talk about the activities they enjoyed and what they have learnt.

Special features of this book:

- **Activity note:** situated at the bottom of every left-hand page, this suggests further activities and encourages discussion about what your child has learnt.

- **Abc panel:** situated at the bottom of every right-hand page, this builds up the phonetic alphabet by showing pictures of words that start with the letter sounds from a to z. Use this to recap the 26 letter sounds in this book.

- **Red letters:** these distinguish between the letter and the sound. In this book the phoneme (letter sound) is shown in **red**.

- **Trace the letter:** talk about the shape of each letter and the movement as your child traces it – anti-clockwise circle and straight up and back down for the letter 'a'. Encourage them to sound out the letter sound each time.

- **Certificate:** the certificate on page 24 should be used to reward your child for their effort and achievement. Remember to give them plenty of praise and encouragement, regardless of how they do.

Published by Collins
An imprint of HarperCollins*Publishers* Ltd
The News Building
1 London Bridge Street
London SE1 9GF

HarperCollins*Publishers*
1st Floor, Watermarque Building,
Ringsend Road, Dublin 4, Ireland

© HarperCollins*Publishers* Ltd 2004
This edition © HarperCollins*Publishers* Ltd 2022

10 9 8 7 6 5 4 3 2 1

ISBN 978-0-00-815150-8

The author asserts the moral right to be identified as the author of this work.

All rights reserved. No part of this publication may be reproduced, stored in a retrieval system, or transmitted, in any form or by any means, electronic, mechanical, photocopying, recording or otherwise, without the prior permission of Collins.

British Library Cataloguing in Publication Data

A Catalogue record for this publication is available from the British Library.

Written by Carol Medcalf
Design and layout by Lodestone Publishing Limited and Contentra Technologies Ltd
Illustrated by Contentra Technologies Ltd
Cover design by Sarah Duxbury and Amparo Barrera
Project managed by Sonia Dawkins and Tracey Cowell
All images are © Shutterstock.com and © HarperCollins*Publishers* Ltd
Printed in India by Multivista Global Pvt. Ltd

MIX
Paper from responsible sources
FSC™ C007454

Contents

How to use this book   2

a   4

b   5

c   6

d   7

e   8

f   9

g   10

h   11

i, j   12

k   13

l   14

m   15

n   16

o   17

p, q   18

r   19

s   20

t   21

u, v, w   22

x, y, z   23

Certificate   24

Answers   Inside back cover

a

- Trace the letter with your finger. Say the a sound.

- Draw lines to match the pictures that start with the a sound to the letter a.

Help your child to name each picture in this activity and sound out the beginning letter. Now try looking around the room to find objects that begin with the a sound. Group them into a pile. Draw the letter 'a' on some paper and place it next to the pile. Repeat the activity for other letter sounds.

b

- Trace the letter with your finger. Say the b sound.

- Trace the path from the letter b to the pictures. What sound do the pictures start with?

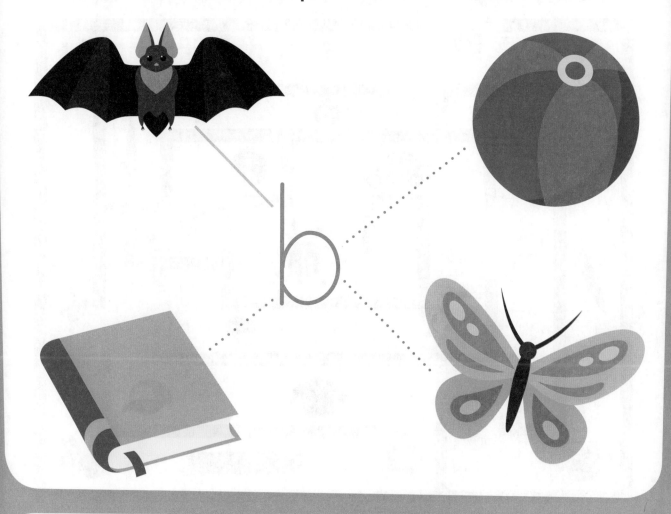

c

- Trace the letter with your finger. Say the c sound.

- Follow the maze from the 🐱 to the 🤡 . Only pass pictures that start with the c sound. What do you pass?

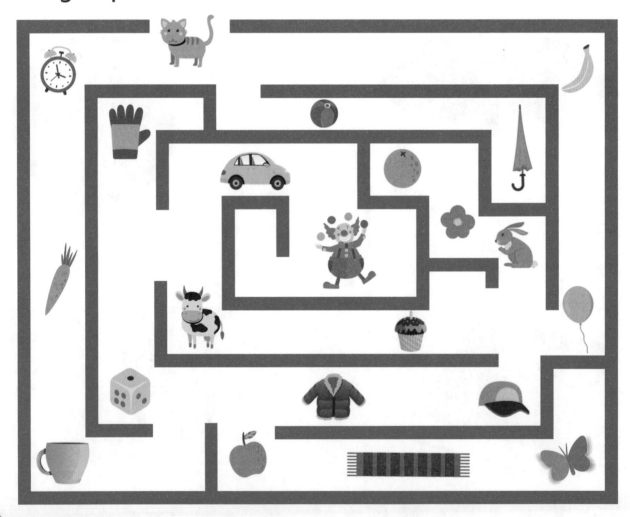

d

- Trace the letter with your finger. Say the d sound.

d

- Find the pictures that start with the d sound.

e

- Trace the letter with your finger. Say the e sound.

- Draw a circle round the pictures that start with the e sound.

Make alphabet shape biscuits using playdough cutters or by rolling the dough into long thin strips and writing the letters. Talk about the letters and their sounds as you play together.

8

f

- Trace the letter with your finger. Say the f sound.

- Colour the pictures that start with the f sound.

g

- Trace the letter with your finger. Say the g sound.

g

- Find the pictures that start with the g sound.

Collect old cards and magazines. Look through them together and find pictures that start with the g sound. Cut them out and make a letter sound collage. Discuss the letter sound and all the pictures that you have stuck down. Repeat the activity for other letter sounds.

● Trace the letter with your finger. Say the h sound.

● Trace the path from the letter h to the pictures. What sound do the pictures start with?

i, j

- Trace the letters with your finger. Say the i and j sounds.

i   j

- Draw lines to match the pictures that start with the i and j sounds to their correct letter.

k

- Trace the letter with your finger. Say the k sound.

k

- Draw a circle round the pictures that start with the k sound.

l

● Trace the letter with your finger. Say the l sound.

● Trace the path from the letter l to the pictures. What sound do the pictures start with?

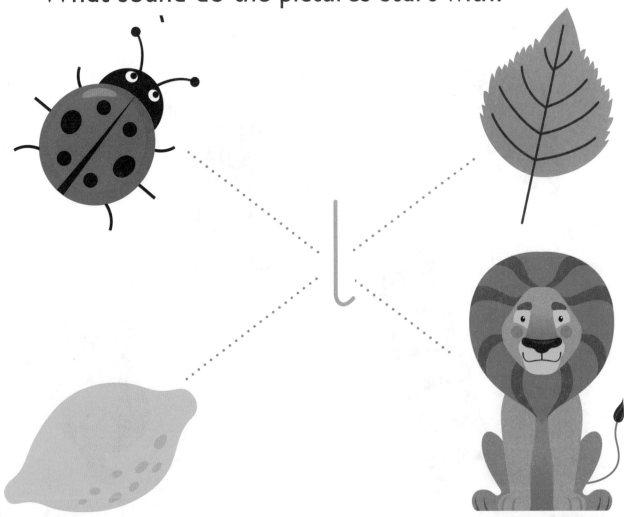

m

Trace the letter with your finger. Say the m sound.

Colour the pictures that begin with the m sound.

n

- Trace the letter with your finger. Say the n sound.

- Draw lines to match the pictures that start with the n sound to the letter n.

Go for a letter sound walk together and make up a story on the way. Your child's name is a good place to start: Davina and Daddy took dolly and their dog to buy donuts. Freddy walked across the field of flowers and saw a frog.

● Trace the letter with your finger. Say the o sound.

● Look at the pictures. What letter sound do they start with? Draw a picture of a word that starts with the same sound in the box below.

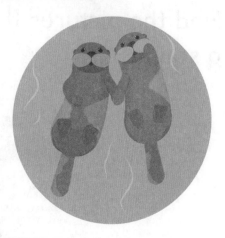

p, q

- Trace the letters with your finger. Say the p and q sounds.

- Find the pictures that begin with the p and q sounds.

When reading together, encourage your child to name the pictures in the book and tell you the letter sounds they start with.

r

- Trace the letter with your finger. Say the r sound.

- Draw a circle round the pictures that start with the r sound.

s

- Trace the letter with your finger. Say the s sound.

s

- Follow the maze from the ⭐ to the ☀.

Only pass pictures that start with the s sound.
What do you pass?

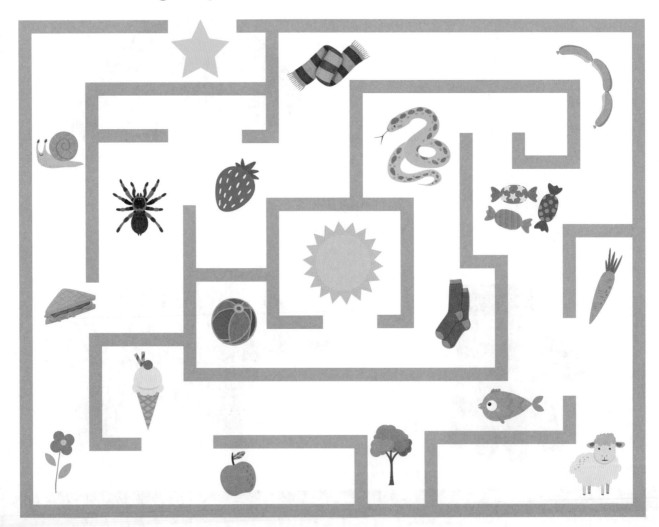

Trace the letter with your finger. Say the t sound.

Trace the path from the letter t to the pictures. What sound do the pictures start with?

u, v, w

- Trace the letters with your finger. Say the u, v and w sounds.

- Draw lines to match the pictures that start with the u, v and w sounds to their correct letter.

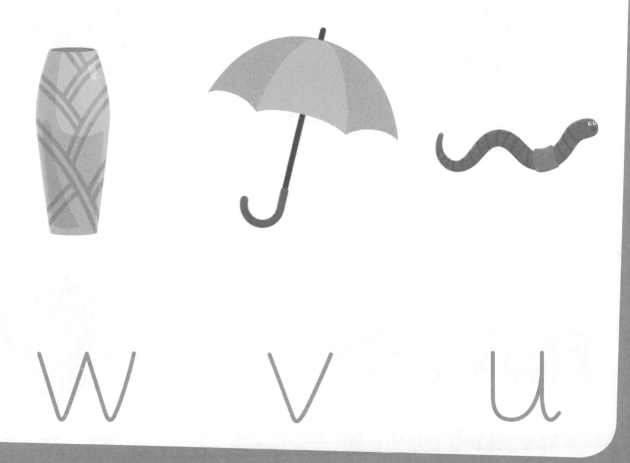

x, y, z

- Trace the letters with your finger. Say the x, y and z sounds.

- Draw an orange (circle) round the picture that starts with the x sound.

  Draw a blue (circle) round the picture that starts with the y sound.

  Draw a yellow (circle) round the picture that starts with the z sound.

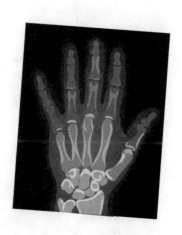  

Well done .... (name)

You have finished!

Now you know all your letters!

Date ....

Age ....